PUFFIN BOOKS
UK | USA | Australia | Canada | India | Ireland | New Zealand | South Africa

Puffin Books is part of the Penguin Random House group of companies
whose addresses can be found at global.penguinrandomhouse.com.

www.penguin.co.uk   www.puffin.co.uk   www.ladybird.co.uk

First published in the US by World of Eric Carle, 2023
Published in the UK by Puffin Books, 2024

001

Printed and bound in China

The authorized representative in the EEA is Penguin Random House Ireland,
Morrison Chambers, 32 Nassau Street, Dublin D02 YH68

A CIP catalogue record for this book is available from the British Library

ISBN: 978–0–241–64987–9

To find out more about Eric Carle and his books, please visit **eric-carle.com**
To learn about The Eric Carle Museum of Picture Book Art, please visit **carlemuseum.org**

All correspondence to: Puffin Books, Penguin Random House Children's,
One Embassy Gardens, 8 Viaduct Gardens, London SW11 7BW

MIX
Paper | Supporting
responsible forestry
FSC® C018179

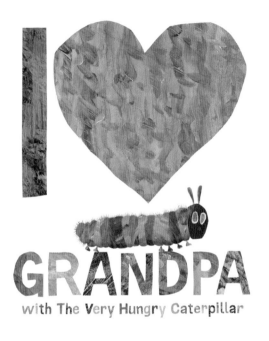

I ♥ GRANDPA

with The Very Hungry Caterpillar

Eric Carle

PUFFIN

Grandpa...

I can always
count on you . . .

to **cheer** me on

and cheer me **up,**

or to make me
laugh.

Even when . . .

I'm feeling

or left out,

you show me you
care,

and make me feel so

special.

That's why...

GRAN

YOU

DPA